HighTide and Ellie Keel Productions
present

COLLAPSIBLE

by Margaret Perry

Collapsible premiered at VAULT Festival, London, on 13 February 2019, before transferring to the Edinburgh Festival Fringe in August 2019 and HighTide Festival, Aldeburgh, in September 2019, co-produced with HighTide. The show subsequently transferred to the Dublin Fringe in September 2019, and the Bush Theatre, London, in February–March 2020.

COLLAPSIBLE

by Margaret Perry

CAST

ESSIE	Breffni Holahan
DEREK	Omar Ibrahim

CREATIVE TEAM

Director	Thomas Martin
Designer	Alison Neighbour
Lighting Designer	Alex Fernandes
Sound Designer	Jon McLeod
Producer	Ellie Keel for Ellie Keel Productions
Associate Producer	Jennifer Lunn for Ellie Keel Productions
Production and Marketing Associate	Gabrielle Leadbeater for Ellie Keel Productions
Production Manager	Nathaniel Lunn and Jack Greenyer
Scenic Artist	Victoria Langoy
Stage Manager	Lucy Morris
Production Photography	Holly Revell
Marketing Photography	Bronwen Sharp
Marketing Design	Martha Hegarty

BIOGRAPHIES

MARGARET PERRY | WRITER
Margaret Perry is a playwright from Cork, living in London. Her plays include *Porcelain* (Abbey Theatre and BBC Radio 4); *I Could Have Danced All Night* (Old Vic Workrooms) and *Every Little*, which was a finalist for Soho Theatre's Tony Craze Award 2019 with a Special Commendation for innovation in theatrical form. She is currently part of a studio writing group at the Royal Court and is under commission at The Yard and the Bush Theatre. She was the recipient of an MGC Futures Bursary to develop *Collapsible*, which won an Origins Award for Outstanding New Work at VAULT Festival 2019. She is a graduate of Drama and Theatre Studies at University College Cork, where she also teaches.

BREFFNI HOLAHAN | ESSIE
Breffni Holahan is a Dublin/London based actress. Theatre credits include work with the Abbey Theatre, BBC/Avalon, Dead Centre, Collapsing Horse, Brokentalkers, Anu Productions, and Rough Magic. In 2015, she co-founded MALAPROP Theatre, devising and performing award-winning productions such as *LOVE+* and *Everything Not Saved*. Screen work includes *The Racer* (Blinder Films); *Vikings* (History Channel/MGM) and *Everything Not Saved* (RTÉ).

THOMAS MARTIN | DIRECTOR
Previous work includes the award-winning *Ross & Rachel* (Edinburgh Fringe Festival/59E59 New York/Battersea Arts Centre/UK tour); *If We Got Some More Cocaine I Could Show You How I Love You* (Old Red Lion/Project Arts Centre/Glor Ennis/Mick Lally Galway/VAULT Festival); *Siren* (Edinburgh Fringe/VAULT Festival); *Bromley, Bedlam, Bethlehem* (Old Red Lion); *Followers* (Southwark Playhouse). Work with young people and nonprofessionals includes *Sing Before You Speak Again* (Young Vic Taking Part) and *Talk Me Down* (Cambridge Junction Young Company). He trained on the National Theatre's Directors Course, was a finalist for the JMK Award, and reads for the National, Bush, and Hampstead Theatres. As the co-founder of Beta Public, London's only night of theatre and video games, he has curated nights at Camden People's Theatre and the V&A.

ALISON NEIGHBOUR | DESIGNER
Alison Neighbour is a scenographer working in theatre, dance, installation, and site-specific environments. Her work includes text based, devised, and self-led projects. She trained at RADA, is represented by The Designer's Formation, and is a resident at Pervasive Media Studio. Alison is also co-founder of Bread & Goose. Recent work includes *The Girl With Incredibly Long Hair* (Wales national tour); *Good Girl* (Trafalgar Studios); *Tumulus* (Soho Theatre/Vaults Festival Origin Award); *The Little Prince* (Playground Theatre); *Hanging in the Balance* (mac, Birmingham); *Constellations & A Peter Rabbit Tale* (Singapore Repertory Theatre); *Ross & Rachel* (UK tour); *Spine* (UK tour); *The Curtain* (Young Vic); *De-Railed* (HOME, Manchester); *Phenomenal People* (Fuel/UK tour); *Crazy Gary's Mobile Disco* (Chapter Arts Centre/Wales tour); *I Told You This Would Happen* (ARC, Stockton/UK tour); *Lost in the Neuron Forest* (Wales Millennium Centre/UK tour); *The Eyes Have It* (Imagine Watford Festival).

ALEX FERNANDES | LIGHTING DESIGNER

Alex Fernandes is a lighting designer for contemporary performance, and was the recipient of the 2013 Michael Northern Bursary. Other lighting work includes *DOMESTICA* (Battersea Arts Centre, UK/international tour); *Super Duper Closeup* (Yard Theatre/UK tour); *Double Double Act* (Unicorn Theatre); *The Drill Project* (The Place, Robin Howard Dance Theatre); *Minor Planets* (HAU Berlin); *Kim Kardashian* (Bale da Cidade de Palmas, Brazil); *Tonight I'm Gonna Be The New Me* (Forest Fringe/UK tour). Alex was the technical director of Forest Fringe in Edinburgh between 2013 and 2016.

JON MCLEOD | SOUND DESIGNER

Credits include; *Icarus* (Unicorn Theatre); *The Picture of Dorian Gray* (UK tour); *The Importance of Being Earnest* (Watermill Theatre); *The Political History of Smack and Crack, Spine* (Soho Theatre); *Carmen The Gypsy* (Arcola Theatre); *If We Got Some More Cocaine I Could Show You How I Love You* (Old Red Lion); *Ross & Rachel* (Battersea Arts Centre); *Macbeth, Followers* (Southwark Playhouse); *Penguinpig, Zeraffa Giraffa* (Little Angel); *Fair Field, Party Skills for the End of The World, 66 Minutes in Damascus, Busking It* (Shoreditch Town Hall); *Tribute Acts* (Camden People's Theatre); *Brutal Cessation, Dark Room* (Theatre503); *Arthur's World, The Rest of Your Life* (Bush Theatre); *Strangers In Between* (Trafalgar Studios); *Food, Just To Get Married, I'm Gonna Pray For You So Hard* (Finborough Theatre); *A Conversation, Stink Foot* (The Yard).

ELLIE KEEL | PRODUCER

Ellie Keel is an independent arts producer with a broad portfolio of theatre productions and events to her name. After two years working for Thelma Holt Ltd, the Oxford Playhouse, and the Cameron Mackintosh Foundation, she now specialises in commissioning and creating successful productions of new plays with her company Ellie Keel Productions. Ellie's work encompasses productions in many London off-West End venues, including Barbican Centre (*Redefining Juliet*), Soho Theatre (*HOTTER*), Arcola (*Callisto: a queer epic; Heretic Voices; Mrs Dalloway; Anna Bella Eema*), the Finborough Theatre (*Home Chat*), Theatre503 (*The Games We Played*), and VAULT Festival (*Collapsible; The D Word*). In 2017 she co-founded Heretic Voices, an international competition to find the best new plays in monologue form. Ellie is also a Creative Associate at The North Wall Arts Centre, where she is the co-founder of the annual Alchymy Festival, a festival showcasing the work of talented early-career theatremakers from across the UK. In addition to her professional productions, Ellie has produced large-scale, site-specific plays with The Big House, a charity working with young people at the risk of social exclusion. Ellie is a Director of LGBT+ youth charity Just Like Us and a Trustee of The King's Hall Trust for the Arts.

GABRIELLE LEADBEATER | PRODUCTION AND MARKETING ASSOCIATE

Gabrielle Leadbetter is an Associate Producer with Ellie Keel Productions. Her credits as an independent producer include *My Mother Runs in Zig-Zags* at the North Wall Arts Centre, *Your Little Play* at the Michael Pilch Studio and *Medea* at the Belgrade Theatre. Gabrielle is also a backstage member of the National Youth Theatre and her Stage Management credits include *The Reluctant Fundamentalist* at Bradford Literary Festival and the Edinburgh Fringe Festival, *Vintage New Year's Party* at the Southbank Centre, *Zigger Zagger* at Wilton's Music Hall, *Twelfth Night* at Middle Temple Hall, and *The Story of our Youth* at the Shaftesbury Theatre.

LUCY MORRIS | STAGE MANAGER

Lucy Morris graduated from the Royal Central School of Speech and Drama in 2018. Her credits include *A Small Place* (Stage Manager, Gate Theatre); the Guilty Feminist's *Suffrageddon* (Stage Manager, tour), and *Salty Irina* (Stage Manager, Ovalhouse). Lucy's work with Ellie Keel Productions includes *In Lipstick* (Stage Manager, The Pleasance) and *Collapsible* (Stage Manager, VAULT Festival). In 2018 Lucy co-founded Ondervinden with Elske Waite, a theatre company focused on retelling traditional stories through unheard perspectives.

HIGH TIDE

NEW THEATRE FOR ADVENTUROUS PEOPLE

HighTide is a theatre company and charity based in East Anglia that has an unparalleled twelve-year history of successfully launching the careers of emerging British playwrights.

Our alumni speak for themselves: Luke Barnes, Adam Brace, Tallulah Brown, E V Crowe, Elinor Cook, Rob Drummond, Thomas Eccleshare, Theresa Ikoko, Branden Jacobs-Jenkins, Eve Leigh, Anders Lustgarten, Joel Horwood, Ella Hickson, Harry Melling, Nessah Muthy, Vinay Patel, Nick Payne, Phil Porter, Beth Steel, Al Smith, Sam Steiner, Molly Taylor, Jack Thorne and Frances Ya-Chu Cowhig.

We have staged productions with the highest quality theatres across the UK, from the Traverse in Edinburgh, to the Royal Exchange in Manchester, Theatre Royal Bath and the National Theatre in London. We discover new talent, provide creative development opportunities for playwrights and other creatives, and stage high quality theatre productions both in our region and nationally through our festivals and touring.

We enable new and underrepresented playwrights to express their visions of contemporary politics and society, demonstrate their creative potential and therein showcase the future of theatre.

BackstageTrust

HIGH TIDE

2019

TWELVE YEARS OF SHAPING THE MAINSTREAM

Our twelfth season under Artistic Director Steven Atkinson, began in February 2019 with Eve Leigh's **The Trick**, directed by Roy Alexander Weise in a HighTide and Loose Tongue co-production. **The Trick** premiered at the Bush Theatre before embarking on an national tour.

In April, **Mouthpiece** by Kieran Hurley, presented by Traverse Theatre in association with HighTide transfered to Soho Theatre after a successful run at Traverse Theatre in December 2018. It will return to Edinburgh in August as part of the Traverse's Edinburgh Festival Fringe 2019 season.

Rust by Kenny Emson, directed by Eleanor Rhode, will be presented in a HighTide and Bush Theatre co-production in June 2019 at the Bush Theatre. **Rust** will transfer to the Edinburgh Festival Fringe before running at HighTide Festival in September 2019.

HighTide, in partnership with Assembly Roxy, launch **Disruption: The Future of New Theatre** as part of the Edinburgh Festival Fringe 2019. **Disruption** will present a curated programme of provocative and contemporary new theatre. Alongside **Rust**, HighTide will co-produce a further four productions: **Pops** by Charlotte Josephine, **Collapsible** by Margaret Perry, **Since U Been Gone** by Teddy Lamb & **Pink Lemonade** by Mia Johnson.

Former HighTide First Commissions Writer Sophie Ellerby will premiere **LIT** in September 2019, directed by Stef O'Driscoll in a HighTide and Nottingham Playhouse co-production. **LIT** will debut at the HighTide Festival before transferring to Nottingham Playhouse.

Finally, HighTide are partnering with **BBC Radio 3** and **BBC Arts** on two new radio plays by HighTide alumni writers Tallulah Brown and Vinay Patel. These plays will be presented at HighTide Festival in 2019 with a live recording to be broadcast later this year.

For full details, visit hightide.org.uk

HIGH
TIDE

HIGHTIDE THEATRE

24a St John Street, London, EC1M 4AY
0207 566 9765 - hello@hightide.org.uk - hightide.org.uk

HighTide Company

Artistic Director Steven Atkinson
Artistic Director Designate Suba Das
Executive Producer Francesca Clark
Executive Producer (Maternity Cover) Rowan Rutter
Producer Robyn Keynes
Assistant Producer Holly White
Festival Producer, Aldeburgh Elizabeth Downie
Marketing and Communications Officer Kathleen Smith

Associate Writers:
Taj Atwal, William Drew, Sonia Jalaly, James McDermott, Yolanda Mercy

Patrons
Stephen Daldry CBE; Sir Richard Eyre CBE; Sally Greene OBE; Sir David Hare; Sir Nicholas Hytner; Sam Mendes CBE; Juliet Stevenson CBE.

BE A FRIEND OF THE FESTIVAL

"There are very talented young playwrights in the UK and if they are lucky they will find their way to HighTide Theatre. I hope you will join me in supporting this remarkable and modest organisation. With your help HighTide can play an even more major role in the promoting of new writing in the UK."

Lady Susie Sainsbury, Backstage Trust

Our Friends are an important part of HighTide. Our benefits include:

- An invite to the Festival programme launch party in Aldeburgh
- An invite to the Artists and Friends Brunch during the Festival
- Dedicated ticket booking service and access to house seats for sold out events

From as little as £10 a month, your contribution will support the Festival in providing:

- Performance tickets to local school children
- Workshops on performance and writing
- The Summer Connect club in Aldeburgh for the next generation of playwrights

All of which we can provide at no cost to local young people, thanks to the generosity of our Friends.

Be a Friend for as little as £10 per month, or become a Best Friend for as little as £25 per month.

To make a one-off contribution, please call our offices on 01728 687110 quoting 'Friends of the Festival', or email **rowan@hightide.org.uk**.

We are thankful to all of our supporters, without whom our work simply would not take place.

HighTide Theatre is a National Portfolio Organisation of the Arts Council England

Leading Partner: Lansons

Trusts and Foundations

Aldeburgh Town Council, Backstage Trust, The Barbara Whatmore Charitable Trust, The Boris Karloff Charitable Foundation, The D'Oyly Carte Charitable Trust, The Fenton Arts Trust, Foyle Foundation, The Golsenscott Foundation, Harold Hyam Wingate Foundation, The Lord Belstead Charitable Trust, National Lottery Awards For All, The Martin Bowley Charitable Trust, Suffolk Community Foundation, The Sumner Wilson Charitable Trust, The Sylvia Waddilove Foundation

Major Funder: Backstage Trust

Best Friends of the Festival: Christopher Bretnall and Julia Nelson Creative Broadcasts Solutions, Tim and Caroline Clark, Jan Hall, Priscilla John, Clare Parsons and Tony Langham, John Rodgers, Leah Schmidt and David Kogan, Dennis and Charlotte Stevenson

Friends of the Festival: Steven Atkinson, Francesca Clark, Elizabeth Downie, Nancy Durrant, Liz Fosbury, Jon Gilchrist, Vinay Patel, Graham and Sue White

Business Sponsors

The Agency, Fisher's Gin

Special Thanks

Lynette Linton, Deirdre O'Halloran (and everyone at the Bush Theatre)
Scarlett Plouviez Comnas (and everyone at the Rosemary Branch)
Gillian Greer, FOH and technical staff at VAULT Festival
Marilyn Ensor and Sally Vaughan at St Agnes Church, Kennington
Mary Higgins
Steven Atkinson at HighTide

The Producers would like to extend a special thanks to Gail McManus at PER for her support, advice, and encouragement, for which we are all extremely grateful.

We would also like to thank our Kickstarter supporters, without whom we could not have made this production:

Al Smith
Alan Mahon
Andrew Hughes
Bertie Darrell
Cecelia Parr
Charles Legere
Chris Schafroth
Claire Gilbert
Colin Grubbs
Darren Sinnott
David Elms
Deirdre O' Halloran
Douglas Schatz
Eleanor Crosswell
Elisabeth Lewerenz
Ell Pitta Bread
Ellena Martin
Emily Collins
Emma
eoqui
Erica Murray
Eszter Kalman
Evangeline Cullingworth
FD
Georgia de Grey
Gill Greer
Hannah
Hannah Bristow
Hannah W
Hilary Bowen-Walsh
Holly Robinson
Jane Martin
Jennifer Lunn
Jessica Dromgoole
Jo Geaney
John Bainbridge
John Beechinor
John O'Donovan
Judith Sijstermans
Kate
Katherine Sziraczky
Katie Hickey

Kickstarter
Kiko Itasaka
Kyle
Laura O'Donovan
Lisa Mc Donough and Ciaran Kelly
Maria
Martha
Mary Cahill and Ivan Perry
Mary Higgins
Matt Neubauer
Matthew Gardner
Maud Dromgoole
Michael J. Kunze
Michelle Perry
Mike Kaloski-Naylor
Mike Ryan
Natasha Kaeda
Nathan Ellis
Niamh Denyer
Nicholas Hall
Pat Ashe
Paul Riordan
Rachel Betts
Richard Speir
Robyn Keynes
Rosa Robson
Rosie Kellett
Sarah England
Sarah Kosar
Sheila Peacock
Sinéad Donnachie
Stephen Kyberd
Steve S
Suzanna Ward
The Creative Fund by BackerKit
Vanessa Kisuule
Vinay Patel
Zoe Hunter-Gordon

COLLAPSIBLE

Margaret Perry

Acknowledgements

So many people have made this play.

To Ellen Buckley, Eleanor Crosswell and The Miniaturists.

To Stella McCabe, Molly McCarthy and everyone at MGC Futures.

To Hannah Hauer-King, Gillian Greer, Maud Dromgoole and Chris Thorpe.

To Sammy Johnson. To Jessica Stewart.

To Steven Atkinson, Robyn Keynes, Francesca Clark, Holly White, Suba Das and everyone at HighTide, our co-conspirators.

To the Abbey Theatre and Dublin Fringe. To Lynette Linton and the whole team at The Bush.

To the creative team of dreams – Alison Neighbour, Alex Fernandes, Jon Mcleod, Jennifer Lunn, Lucy Morris, Gabrielle Leadbeater, Martha Hegarty, Omar Ibrahim.

To Ellie Keel, an absolute powerhouse. To the astonishing Breffni Holahan. To Thomas Martin, who is as brilliant as he is delightful and has pushed this script to be the very best version of itself. This play is as much all of yours as it is mine.

And to Deirdre O'Halloran, who believed in this play from the very start and champions my writing at every turn.

THANK YOU.

M.P.

To my friends and family,
who keep me sane

'...a woman who lived well, lived well, lived well, lived on the uppermost layer of the sands of the world, and the sands had never caved in beneath her feet...[until] without warning, there was the loud sound of something solid that suddenly crumbles.'

The Passion According to G.H.,
Clarice Lispector

Character

ESSIE, *a woman*

Some Notes on Production

This a piece for one actor playing one character. We see all the other characters through Essie recalling them for us. I have included quite a lot of 'I say' and 'she/he says' lines that I think make the piece clearer to read, but many of which won't be necessary in performance. If it's clear who's speaking, cut them.

*** indicates scene transitions which should be marked with sound, or movement, or both.

This text went to press before the end of rehearsals and so may differ slightly from the play as performed.

ESSIE. I spend a lot of time on the internet. Especially lately.

The internet knows me so well. The internet tells me which cute animal I am (lamb). Which John Hughes movie I am (*Pretty in Pink*). Which classic car I am (Cadillac). Which roasted meat I am (lamb). Which sandwich I am (BLT). Which major European city I am (Paris). Which condiment I am (mustard). Which element on the Periodic Table I am (neon). Which type of rabbit I am (dwarf). Which US President I am (Nixon. Nixon? I try again. Obama). The internet tells me I'm a Miranda, a Ravenclaw, a Mulan, a Laura Palmer. A dog person, a beach person, a winter person, a cupcake person, a martini person, a lake person, a bird person. The internet tells me I'm an introvert. The internet tells me I'm an extrovert. The internet tells me I sometimes like to go out and sometimes to stay in.

And then there's this video I've watched over and over again, of this 1950s housewife on LSD. Back then they were doing clinical trials on humans, and this housewife, meek and shy as they come, has volunteered, and they've chosen her because she's undergone psychological testing and been found to be a stable, normal person. This doctor sits her down and explains everything and gives her a glass of water with a tiny measure of lysergic acid in it. She drinks it down and he waits a bit and then starts to ask her questions. And there's this one moment – this one – this one moment that I can't forget where he says, 'Mary, how do you feel?' And she says, 'I don't understand the question.' And he points to her and says, 'How do *you* feel?' And she smiles this serene smile. 'Why, doctor,' she says, 'There is no *me*. There is no *you*.' Like it's the most obvious thing in the entire world. And she looks so happy, so light.

And that's where the video ends but I always imagine her when the LSD wears off, putting on her coat and her scarf like ballast, trying to weigh herself back down.

***

It started like this. I lost my job.

Not my fault I just. Never mind.

My sister's arranged to meet me for dinner and I know it's because Mum's asked her to check up on me but I go anyway to prevent further questions, and also because, food. She's brought The Boyfriend. I've not ordered very much because it's not clear if they're going to pay for my meal or if I am. I'm eating my meal very slowly so as not to reveal how small it is and Maura says, are you not hungry Essie, and I say not really which is a lie, I'm always hungry, my metabolism could enter the Olympics if there was a category for metabolisms which of course, there isn't.

So Essie. What's going on with you?

Not much.

Mum says you haven't been answering her calls.

I've been really busy.

Right.

Maura chews. Swallows.

Anyway, I just wanted to check in, see if you're alright?

Pause.

Look up at her worried face and that's when I say it, I don't know what possesses me to say it but I say:

I feel like a chair.

Long pause.

The Boyfriend, Derek he's called, she's had him surgically attached, stares down at his menu even though we ordered ages ago.

What's that? You feel like what?

Eh –

A chair?

Never mind, I just –

Like, that chair, there?

She points to a nearby empty chair, dark wood, a trendy, aloof chair.

Not exactly like that one, no.

Derek's listening now. I can't look at his punchable face.

What – sort of chair, then, is it that you feel like?

Like, one of those folding chairs, you know?

A deckchair.

Not a deckchair.

Pause.

More like, you know, sort of a garden – chair?

A sun lounger?

One of those chairs you can fold and unfold. I say. Those collapsible chairs. Solid one minute and then.

She's shrinking back from me. The stretch of table between us widens and deepens into a canyon.

Now Maura's looking at the menu but Derek's looking at me. Her hand on his wrist, wrapped tight as his watch.

Derek, would you please get the bill.

He's staring at me.

Derek!

Mmm, he says, yeah. He turns for a waiter.

They pay for my tiny meal. I wish I'd known. I'd have had steak.

***

Liz tells me about the new couch she's ordered from Sweden where they really know about design. She tells me about a holiday she's booking with her most recent squeeze, someone called Hayley who works in travel so she's getting them a great deal on one of those hotels where you just press a button and a person appears holding a cocktail.

What's that smell, Liz?

Fennel and cracked sea salt.

She gestures to a huge candle burning in the window.

Wow.

It's this new thing I've started doing. I buy myself something nice once a week, something I don't really need, that's just for me. With the world the way it is, I think it's really important to practise self-care, don't you?

I –

Are you taking care of yourself, Essie?

Course.

Good. It's so important to make time to do something for you. Get a pedicure. Have a bath. It all matters. It's all political, isn't it.

Political?

Yes. How we live, it's politicised, of course it is.

Leave it, I think, leave it but then –

What political statement does having a bath make?

What?

I just mean, don't you think that's a bit convenient? Doing something for yourself, and saying it's political? Buying a – *candle* – and saying it's political? So that you don't have to actually do anything real in the world, for other people?

Pause.

Do you have to shit on literally everything, Essie?

Pause.

Sorry.

Pause.

She moves protectively towards the fennel candle, and blows it out. I'm not worthy of its majesty.

I've known Liz my whole life and I sometimes think we are only friends now because we have been friends for so long.

But she knows me. She knows me and that is – I want to hang on to that.

Liz. I've got a question for you.

Fire away.

What do you think I'm like?

What?

Like if someone asked you, oh, what's Essie like –

Yeah?

What would you say?

I dunno, she says. Come on, Es, you know what you're like.

Course, I say. Course I do. But I have to, sell myself, you know, for my job applications, and I'm running out of things to say. So I've decided to make a list. Crowdsource it from people who know me.

YES, she says.

What?

YES! I like it. It's innovative, it's proactive. You're taking control, Es. I'm happy for you.

Pause.

I'd say you were practical. No-nonsense, she says, a no-nonsense girl with your feet firmly on the ground.

Thanks.

Anything to help you with the job hunt. How are you – *managing*?

I have all the money I saved for the trip.

I was going to go travelling. A year-long holiday. But we didn't call it that, she and I. We called it an adventure. We're going on an adventure, we'd say to each other, bouncing flights and hostels back and forth in snatched moments between meetings and from laptop to laptop side by side in bed. Holidays were for other people; other people went on holiday; but we had adventures.

When I get home, I open my notebook. I write my name on the top of the page and underneath it I write –

Practical. No-nonsense. Feet firmly on the ground.

I tear the page out. I speak the words to the empty room and I like how they sound marching out of my mouth, bright and clear.

Practical. No-nonsense. Feet firmly on the –

***

Esther? If you'd like to come through?

The room is full of lilies in tall vases. Like someone really elegant has died.

Hope you didn't have any trouble finding us! We're a little bit tucked away up here.

No trouble.

Now, before we start, Esther, I want to reassure you that we're not like other companies. And so this won't be like other interviews. We're like a family. There's no hierarchy, here. In this room, we are equals. You're just as much interviewing me, as I am interviewing you. So. I just thought we'd have a little chat. Get to know each other a little better. Could you tell me briefly why you left your last job?

Everyone said I was a fool, that I'd done well to land a permanent position in a company people the world over would kill to work for. Hammering down the doors, they were, making work for the cleaners who started two hours earlier than everyone else to polish their handprints off the glass in the foyer. Did I think I was too good for it? Didn't I like the free fruit baskets? I certainly ate them, didn't I. I certainly ate them.

I stuck at it, because I have been taught never to give up on anything. We love you Esther, they said. Keep doing what you're doing, but do it more. I stuck at it, the weeks rolling on like the cakes for people's birthdays. Do it more and more and more and more. Here's a big smile. Here's a small pay rise. I stuck at it until I'd been there five years and catching sight of my face in the mirror was like seeing an old friend from school that you really meant to stay in touch with.

I was ready for a change.

There's a faint buzzing in the room.

Well, she says, it would certainly be a change. I suppose what I'm wondering is, why do you think you'd be a good fit for us? If you could tell me, in your own words.

I gaze over her shoulder at some lilies and notice a bee perched on the stem.

Practical.

I'm practical. I think I'd really fit in somewhere with a hands-on, can-do approach.

And why do you think that's us?

It says so on your website. 'We pride ourselves on our hands-on, can-do approach.'

Well, she says. We outsource our website copy to a brand consultancy. I suppose, she says, what I'm getting at is – it looks from your CV that this role would be a bit of a step down for you, in terms of your career trajectory. Can you tell me why you're not a little bit overqualified for this job?

No-nonsense.

Well I probably am a bit overqualified. But that means I'd be able to get straight down to work, hit the ground running.

She's nodding.

I mean, I could do this job in my sleep. And I really need the money.

The buzzing stops.

The bee drops off the lily, lands on to the table, the soft thud of a small fist.

***

Well, it's nice to see you.

What do you want?

Jack's lips are a disc-drive slit.

Oh, I –

You ghost me months ago and now you suddenly want a coffee?

Eh. Yeah.

Bit fucking rude.

You're here though. I say.

Only out of morbid curiosity. You dropped off the face of the earth. Thought you might have died.

Right, well, sorry to disappoint. I'll get right to it.

I'm making a list of words, that describe me? And since you know me pretty well – used to, I mean, I wondered if you had anything to add to it.

He looks at it.

Fuck's this?

It's just research, for my interviews.

You're getting interviews then?

Yeah. Tons.

That's good, he says in a really angry voice.

Pause.

You're a militant perfectionist. But don't tell them that's your greatest weakness, they've heard that a million times. Have you got a weakness prepared?

I'm in the process of choosing one from the platter. He laughs like you might laugh at the joke of an elderly relative and sort of pats my arm.

He looks at the list again.

This is really weird, Essie.

Nah, it's just – something to keep me busy.

Why can't you just binge-watch a series like a normal person.

Pause.

I have to wee.

In the bathroom I touch the skin on my cheek and it feels like somebody else's skin.

***

Can't get the sliver of it out of my head. The way she used to look at me when I came home at the end of the day. I don't miss anything about her except for that. And you can get that with a dog, too. The way they look up when you come through the door.

I'm watching my dad eat a kebab.

Very good-quality meat in this, Esther. Do you want a bite?

No thanks.

Very nice place this. Very friendly staff.

No need to sound so surprised.

What are these green things?

Peppers.

They're very nice.

I'm glad Dad. What time's your flight tomorrow?

10 a.m., he says. I've only just got here and you're already counting down the minutes till you can get rid of me!

He wipes his mouth.

How're your job applications going, love?

Okay. I've been getting interviews.

Oh I'm so relieved! He says. Give them your all, won't you.

Yeah Dad, I will.

Give them everything you've got.

I will.

I mean it now. Go in there with absolutely everything you've got.

He lowers his voice.

Are you – you know – managing? Financially?

Yeah. I'm okay.

Well that's great to hear! Because – well I must say –

What?

When you said you wanted to meet up, your mother and I – we thought you might need money.

Because that's the only reason I'd ever want to see you, is it.

Course not love. Course not! Just you sounded urgent, on the phone, you sounded – not quite yourself.

Oh?

I was worried. We both were, I mean, we are, worried.

Well here I am. I say. Myself.

Exactly. He smiles at me. Let's enjoy the evening then. Will I order some wine?

We sink into the night and I am trying to be in it with him.

Any ladies on the scene Esther?

No Dad.

Men?

No Dad.

You should think about getting a dog, he says. A dog would be great company for you.

My landlord won't even let me put posters up.

A small one, he says. No trouble, the small ones.

Plus I can't afford a dog.

They don't eat much, the small ones.

Okay Dad.

Pause.

He rummages in his coat pocket.

Listen, I should start heading back to the hotel. Before I forget – give this to your sister next week, will you.

Oh, it's beautifully wrapped –

Your mother wrapped it. It's a descaler.

A what.

A descaler. For her kettle. The water over here is extremely tough on kettles and it really affects the quality of the cup of tea you'd get.

I'm not sure if I'll see her on her birthday, actually –

Course you will, he says.

Pause.

Dad –

Yeah?

Casual, like it's a throwaway question.

There was something I wanted to ask you, actually, before you go.

Go on then.

If you were to describe me in one word, what would that word be?

What a funny question.

Humour me.

Pause.

Smart, he says. You've always been clever. All those good marks. It's a gift, that. You can do anything you put your mind to. Absolutely anything. Don't forget it.

Thanks, Dad.

Enjoy it, he says. That's your ration of compliments for the year.

***

It got tricky, with her, to remember where I stopped and she started. I'd sometimes forget whose limbs were whose, waking up sleepy to scratch my leg and she'd ask what I was doing and could I please cut my nails. Joked once about wanting to find a zip in her skin, climb into it and wear it over my own.

Can't work out if that's sweet, or a bit *Silence of the Lambs*.

Imagine. It'd be like one of those rain ponchos you get at festivals.

You're such a freak, Es.

Now you know.

I already knew.

She runs a finger down my spine.

Come here you.

***

When I wake up there's a strange body in my bed. I look down at it and tell myself it's mine. Tell myself I am lying in it. A shadow in clear water.

Maura's hosting what she's insisting on calling an 'intimate gathering' for her birthday. Sounds like an *Eyes Wide Shut* party, I told her, and I refuse to attend a sex party with an immediate family member. But here I am, late and clutching a descaler.

You're wearing it!

The brooch I made her is splashed on her chest, gold silk against her black dress.

Course I am, it's beautiful. You could sell these, I'm telling you.

I just smile.

I'm serious! Derek could help you with the marketing, get a website set up, all that. Couldn't you babe?

He's standing at her shoulder eating a nacho like an awkward sentinel.

Yeah, I mean that's all pretty entry-level stuff, but I'd be happy to.

You should really think about it. You could make real money from these.

I don't want to sell them. That's not the point.

What is the point then?

They're just for fun.

Fun! That's your youth talking. I don't have time to do anything fun any more.

Wordlessly, Derek hands her a margarita.

I'm just at a stage in my life when I need to focus on my career before it's too late, you know and –

Derek puts on some nondescript electronica and starts sort of nodding to it, like he's politely agreeing with himself.

There just only is so much time, Es, as a woman to really *establish* yourself, to, I suppose really *leave your mark* – The door pings.

I'll be right back.

Pause.

Drink, Essie? Derek says.

Please.

Pause.

How are you, anyway?

Fine.

Good, that is very good.

Pause.

How's the job hunt going?

Fine. Fine.

Don't mention the war!

What?

You'll find something. I know you will. Maura tells me you're very driven, Essie. A real self-starter.

Thanks. My hand reaches for the list, folded in my pocket.

He raises his empty wine glass to his lips and takes a sip of air.

Listen, we should go for a coffee.

His tone is light and breezy, like this is a perfectly normal occurrence, like we often spend time just the two of us when in fact the last time was at Maura's summer barbecue when she had to run to the shop for ice and Derek and I spent an excruciating twenty minutes trying to introduce people we did not know to each other.

Maybe on Saturday? He says. I'd love to give you a hand setting up that website.

Maura must have told him to make more of an effort with me. That's exactly the sort of thing she'd do.

I know this place near you actually, they do a lovely Scotch egg.

Oh. Oh that's nice of you but I've actually got plans, on Saturday.

Right. He says. No problem.

Some other time, maybe.

Yeah. Course.

Maura comes back in trailed by two devastatingly beautiful women and I head towards her holding her gift out in front of me like I'm one of the three wise men.

Oh Es, she says, there was no need!

It's actually from Dad.

How was Dad, the other day? Maura says.

Fine.

How's his knee?

Oh. Not sure. I didn't ask.

***

In the mornings I read the list aloud to myself. Send the words skyward.

Practical. No-nonsense. Perfectionist. Smart. Driven. A self-starter. Feet firmly on the ground.

A friend from my old job says I'm bubbly. I picture bits of me rising into my head and evaporating through my scalp.

You were the life and soul of the office! Friday-night drinks just aren't the same without you.

When I ask for tap water he pours some of his sparkling into my glass without saying anything.

You left so suddenly! We didn't even get a chance to do a card. I can put in a good word with Rachel, he says, if you'd want to come back.

No thank you.

I don't really know why you left in the first place if I'm honest, Esther, he says.

They let me go.

His face sags. It's funny to watch. I watch myself in my chair watching his face.

I had heard that. But I didn't believe it! Why, if you don't mind me asking?

Because well I sort of gradually started to notice that I was stones.

Sludgy silt gathering first on my tongue. Grit in my teeth. Spit black in the sink at night. Went to the dentist and she said it was plaque, but then the pebbles started forming, small and wave-washed smooth and I started to rattle slightly when I walked. And at first I just put my clothes over my skin and my coat over my clothes and left the house like nothing was wrong like I wasn't actually a skin-bag full of stones.

But the stones kept piling higher. When they reached my chest it got difficult to get up in the morning, I mean that literally, I wanted to get up and out the door but a large quantity of small stones really weighs a surprising amount and it was an enormous effort even to sit up. And so I started to stay in bed and when I did manage to haul myself into the office the stones sort of sat behind my eyes in a passive-aggressive pile and made everything a bit grey round the edges and that made it quite difficult to see my screen or listen in meetings or really just get any work done. And that's when I stopped coming to work altogether and when I'd used up all my sick days and then some, they had to very gently, very tactfully, let me go.

We love you Esther, they said and when you love someone, you let them go.

I say, contract was up and they decided not to renew it. Probably so they didn't have to increase my salary, the bastards.

I hope you're keeping busy?

As a bee.

Fun fact, he says, did you know that bees are not actually that busy? A recent study in a Chinese province that replaced bees with people found conclusively, Esther it found *absolutely conclusively* that a person can pollinate flowers at a considerably quicker rate than a bee can. People don't waste time faffing around between each flower, you see. They just get on with it.

He pushes his glasses up his nose.

What a time to be alive.

On the bus home I add the word to the list.

Bubbly.

***

Practical. No-nonsense. Perfectionist. Smart. Driven. A self-starter. Bubbly.

Take a seat Esther, you're right on time! I hate the early ones, you know, ten, fifteen minutes early, too keen! Go and have a cup of fucking coffee or something, you know what I mean, take a walk around the shitting, block, a few times, right? Anyway it's great to meet you, I'm Dan and this is Kelly, she's sitting in as a member of HR.

Hi Dan. Hi Kelly. It's great to be here, I'm so excited!

Dan slaps his hands on his knees. Good stuff. Great stuff. Lovely stuff. So! You want to come and join us here in the trenches.

Can you tell us a little bit about yourself?

Pause.

Well. I bring an upbeat positive energy to any workplace, I like to keep things light, have some fun around the office, I mean not too much fun obviously we're here to work but I'd say I'm – bubbly.

Bubbly. Dan says.

Yeah. Yes but I'm also very focused, very driven. I'm a real self-starter. I get things off the ground. I make things happen.

Kelly smiles. Can you tell us a little more about that?

Well I think if you want something to happen you can't just sit around, can you. You've got to work for it.

They're nodding like bobble-head dogs.

I mean if you want something you've got to go after it, if you want something to change or be fixed or get better or stop hurting you have to *drive forward towards that thing*, I think, and that's what I'm. Well that's something I. Do.

Long pause.

Kelly's looking at my CV.

Esther I can see here that you've been out of work for a little while, is that right?

Her voice is kind.

That must be tough. Could you tell us a little about what you've been doing with your time?

Well. I say. I've been job-hunting.

Job-hunting can really feel like a job in itself, can't it!

If only it paid!

Dan darts a glance at Kelly. Then he picks up his pen and moves it from the left- to the right-hand side of the desk in a careful, deliberate movement.

***

I thought we needed to have a bit of a chat.

Liz has brought me out for lunch. She's insisted on paying. I'm really focused on my steak, sharp knife gliding through the rare flesh.

Essie?

Mm. Yeah. I say.

I'm worried about you.

Chew. Oh?

I've watched you mope around for months now, and I think you need to start changing your outlook. Invest in yourself. You'd be surprised how much it might help.

I put down my steak knife.

You need to think about what you want, Essie. What do *you really want*?

I want to be tiny.

I want to be nowhere.

Pause.

Swallow.

I don't know.

Pause.

You need to start making some plans, Es. Like, what you're going to do when your savings run out. Have you thought about that at all?

Yeah –

And? What are you going to do?

Get a job. Any job. Do that job until I'm eighty. Then die I guess?

Oh here we go.

She puts down her fork.

What?

Nothing, she says. Trying to button it back in but it's spilling out all over her face.

If you've got something to say to me, just say it.

Alright then. I will. I want you to grow the fuck up.

Pause.

Grow up and get over yourself. We're not nineteen any more, Es and I've had just about enough.

Is that right, I say.

You think you're so much better than everyone else, than me and the rest of us with our boring jobs and our pension plans, you think you're *above* all of that. You always have. Do you know how many people would have *killed* to work at that company? And you just walked away from it. You think we're all sheep and you're some kind of miraculous fucking giraffe stood in the middle looking down on us.

I –

You think I haven't noticed you sneering at me every time I tell a story about my work, because I actually enjoy my job and get on with my colleagues, heaven forbid! And yeah, what I do isn't rocket science. It's not brain surgery. But do you know what, my job lets me have a nice life and at least I'm contributing something to the world instead of sat on my ass all day every day thinking about *myself*. You know you haven't asked me once about me or how I am in the last six months? Not once.

I.

Pause.

That's not true.

Pause.

Well go on then, how are you?

She's quivering.

I'm not great, as it happens. Hayley dumped me while we were on holiday, right in the middle of the holiday so that was pretty shit.

Her arms are folded tight like she's holding her heart in.

I scrabble around in the air.

I don't know what to say – I've been, well it's just –

What?

It's just that – I don't know if anything I say is real. If anything I do, is real. It's like one day I woke up and noticed that everything's hollow and now I can't unsee it, I can't go back. Every gesture is empty, like – a bowl full of air.

Like, if I do something nice, I worry that what other people might observe in me as a consideration for people's feelings, as kindness, is completely wrapped up in my own desire for people to see me as kind, as considerate. I'm afraid that everything I have ever done for someone else has been about me. About trying to control the way I am viewed in the world. I'm forever saying sorry and it looks like a haste to make sure that I haven't caused offence – that's good, right? That's decent. Wrong. What I'm doing, what I'm doing really is checking that my own image is still intact in the mind of the other person. Even this thought has originated from the worry that other people may think I am using them as a kind of mirror. Even this thought is about me.

I'll tell you what I really want. I want to step out of my body like it's a suit I rented at a costume shop. I want to jump clean out of my brain.

It's just what, Essie?

It's just – well that's shit, about Hayley. But don't you think it could be so much worse?

Don't you think there are lots of things happening in the world right now that are so much worse?

Pause.

So really, you're lucky, Liz. Don't you ever stop to think about how lucky you are?

Pause.

She starts to cry, almost completely silently, tears streaming down her face. She waves for the waiter. She pays for both our meals. She leaves a fifteen per cent tip. She takes a tissue from her bag and dabs her face, checks her make-up.

She looks at me.

She goes.

***

I thought Sandy, for the right one.

Sandy?

It suits. Don't you think it suits?

Sounds like a dog's name.

What about Sandy from *Grease*?

You want to name my right knee after Sandy from *Grease*?

It's got that vibe. Like it might at any moment come of age and start to dress in leather.

Does it, she says.

Trust me. And for the left one – Brendan.

Brendan. Fucking – Brendan?

You promised. You promised I could name them anything I wanted.

And this is what you've chosen.

It's a good, dependable name, Brendan. Can't go wrong.

I think we've already gone wrong, she says. I think something went wrong around the time you requested to name my knees?

Elbows next week.

Listen, can I take you back to the shop? Any chance of a full refund?

Fuck off.

As if, she says. Sure what would you do without me.

***

I'm looking at some exposed brick thinking I know how it feels. The list is clamped in my sweaty hand, paper worn thin and shiny now.

Essie?

Caroline calls to me from a table for two. She's wearing a new coat, snug and glossy and I'm so thrown by that when I sit down I open my mouth to say hello and what comes out is

How's your coat

What, she says.

Your coat. It's new.

Oh this? I've had this for a while.

It's nice.

Thanks.

Pause.

Sorry I'm late. I walked past this place twice. What's with the medicine sign out front?

It's been converted from an old 1960s pharmacy, she says.

But how are people supposed to know it's a café?

I dunno. I guess they just sense it?

She raises an eyebrow at me and I crack a smile. Then stop. Remember.

Pause.

How have you been, Essie?

Yeah good.

Keeping busy?

As a bee.

I saved a bee's life the other day, she says. It was lying on the doorstep on its back sort of, flailing. I'd had a long day and I thought about just walking past it but then I thought, look at this poor defenceless creature. Gave it a spoonful of sugar and water and it perked right up.

Not defenceless. I say. Famously.

Pause.

So –

So –

Sorry, she says. You go.

Eh. Okay, well. I'm making a list of words, that describe me? And I wondered if you had any to add.

My hand trembles as I take it out of my pocket and show her.

It's for my job interviews.

Pause.

What is this?

I told you. It's a list of words that describe me.

Pause.

This could be anyone, Essie.

At the table opposite it is a child's birthday and he is crying because the helium balloon tied around his finger is too tight. His mother is trying to unpick the knot.

She's reading it again.

There are so many words on here, Caroline says, it could describe absolutely anyone.

Pause.

Why are you doing this?

The boy's finger is free. The balloon floats up to the rafters, clings to the roof. He studies the sharp red welt the string has left.

This worries me.

Pause.

I still care about you, she says.

Well you should stop. Caring.

I'd love to Essie, I really would love to but it's not that easy.

Seemed pretty easy before.

The waitress comes and asks if we are finished with our tiny coffees. We nod and she takes away the cups and now we have not even the posture of drinking coffees, now we are just two people having a hard and intense conversation in a refurbished pharmacy.

Can you give it back? I say. The list.

Pause.

Do you really want to talk about this, Essie?

Don't you?

No. Caroline says.

I came here today to tell you that I've forgiven you.

Pause.

I've forgiven you and I want you to be happy. I think given the circumstances, that is more than you should reasonably expect.

Pause.

That is more than you should reasonably expect given that you seem to have forgotten that you smashed up our living room.

Pause.

You seem to have forgotten that you threw a plate at my head. You seem to have forgotten our trip to A&E.

Pause.

Have you. Forgotten. She says.

Pause.

Something lifted and you saw me under it. Maggots under a stone.

GIVE

IT

BACK

Pause.

She's putting on her new coat that's a little too tight under the arms. I start to put on my coat and we're in a race now, who can get it on quicker, who can leave the other sitting alone at this table, my coat is old and well-worn which is giving me a competitive edge.

She puts the list down on the table.

She's turning for the door, her shiny trenchcoat halfway to her shoulders like a crumpled person trying to hitch a ride on her back.

I heard about this service recently, she says. Called a rage room. You pay by the hour to hire a room to go and smash stuff with a baseball bat. Padded walls, you can scream as much as you like.

Caroline –

Pause.

She looks at me.

Take care of yourself, Essie.

***

I'm standing in an open-plan-office warehouse conversion.

Robert Decking, CEO, is sitting on an orange bean bag. He pats an adjacent bean bag in teal.

You must be Esther.

Hello, I say, it's lovely to meet you.

You know who I am.

Yes, I say, I wasn't expecting, I thought I'd be meeting a HR person –

That's not how we do things here, Esther. We've got a more personal approach.

He smiles a wide canyon smile.

I sit. I try to cross my legs, then remember I'm wearing a skirt. I hug my knees, then feel like a toddler. I settle for bending them to one side and await the pins and needles.

Welcome, he says, to the home of innovation and disruption!

I gaze over his shoulder at his Nespresso machine.

Thanks.

I just thought we'd have a chat. Get to know each other a little better.

I've read your CV and I'm a big fan, so you can relax! I suppose I'm just, well if I'm honest, it was the strangest thing, because you've got all this experience, you know project-management experience out the wazoo, for your age Esther it's really impressive – but I'm reading and it strikes me that I'm not sure I can see *you* in it, you know, who *you* are.

Oh. I say.

Because we're looking for individuals here. Singular minds. Dynamic trailblazers. You know? And so I wonder if, first of all, if you could tell me who Esther Nutting *really* is. Let's start with this one – what you think your greatest strength is? Forgive me the ol' tried-and-tested question, ha ha, but I think it's a great one.

Smart.

What's that? he says.

I'm smart. I can do anything I put my mind to.

Pause.

He grins me his piano-key fillings.

I like that you're owning it, Esther, that's what we like to see here, we're after that kind of balls-to-the-wall confidence, if you'll forgive the phrase in the presence of a lady! And now for the second question – what about your greatest weakness?

I'm a perfectionist. A militant perfectionist.

He shifts his weight. The beans crash around like the sea.

Is that right? And why do you think that's a weakness?

I'm opening my mouth before I've had a chance to think. I'm opening my mouth and the stones are there. Waiting smooth and black on my tongue.

Because I'm never satisfied. I run myself ragged, I can't stop until I've given everything I've got, until everything I do is perfect and not just perfect according to me but objectively, actually perfect.

The stones are tumbling out like hail, raining down on the glass coffee table –

It's like – there are structures in the world that say who's the best and who is just average and I want everything I do to be the best by every metric, even new metrics that still haven't been invented. I need it to be. Otherwise, I don't see the point in doing it. Otherwise I don't see the point in doing anything. If perfection isn't achievable I'd rather do nothing. I'd rather do nothing at all than something almost great.

Pause.

Robert Decking, CEO, mimes falling off his bean bag.

Well, he says, I'm floored.

Pause.

I'd love to offer you the position, Esther.

Pause.

I look at his hand, meaty outstretched.

I expect you must have some questions for me.

I stand up on legs full of fizzing static.

I run.

***

ESTHER

Practical

No-nonsense

Perfectionist

Smart

Driven

Self-starter

Bubbly

Feet firmly on the ground

Text my mum Mum what am I like. She says I'm personable, tell them you're personable that's a good word she says people like people who are personable she says. Thanks I say, and she replies saying something else but I don't reply instead I Email an old school friend. Shy, she says, I always thought you were a bit shy, if I'm honest, sorry what's this for again? Ring my primary-school principal. Outgoing, he says, you'd chat to anyone, I remember, nice to hear from you Call an old boss. A team player he says, if you ever need a reference I'd be happy to

ESTHER

Practical

No-nonsense

Perfectionist

Smart

Driven

Self-starter

Bubbly

Personable

Shy

Outgoing

A team player

Feet firmly on the ground

I read it again. Again. Again. Again. Again. Again.

***

I shorten my commute. Bedroom to kitchen to living room to kitchen to bedroom. I am not a recluse – I have to eat. I become a tide, inching out to the corner shop and ebbing back with floating jetsam, crisps and milk and beans. I build a tiny kingdom and watch my savings dribble away like the weeks.

I spend a lot of time on the internet. The internet tells me everything that's happening. All of the carnage, the dead children, the drowned parents, the families fleeing wholesale in a boat underneath a coach on the back of a truck towards a border just waiting to turn them away. The floods and storms and droughts and hurricanes, the planet bucking like a horse trying to throw us all off and out into space, trying to warn us to stop doing what we're doing but we keep doing it, we do it more and more and more and more and this morning Steven Bradley fifty-seven found dead next to a pile of freshly printed CVs his benefits had recently been cut the tusks off and sell them on the black market the white rhino has become officially extinct with the death of the last female in existence and hi @skycustomer service my modem has still not arrived missing for two weeks and vulnerable please share his family want him home safe and well Friday's here and we're giving away a weekend for two in the telephone lines are down in Puerto Rico and our daughter has lost contact with us can you PayPal here to help to help to help by donating to our Kickstarter our GoFundMe you can be part of something that matters.

I sit in my room and read the news, watch the news, livestream the news. If I could I'd pay monthly for an intravenous drip of news. Maybe if it went straight into my blood I would feel it.

I watch hedgehogs being washed cats falling asleep ducklings learning to swim dogs playing pianos children playing with dogs. I watch people doing their make-up doing their weekly shop doing their taxes doing their best in front of the judges and then I find myself back watching Mary tell the doctor she feels she is a normal person, at least her husband certainly thinks so and then the LSD goes down the hatch and her face, the way her face slowly changes like dawn across a kitchen floor and that one that one moment –

Why, doctor. There is no me. There is no you.

There is no me. There is no you.

There is no me. There is no you.

There is no me. There is no you.

I drift off and when I wake I reach for the list and it's not there.

I look in my pockets my bags my bed my floor my drawers my pillowcase and it is not anywhere.

I look again and I am not anywhere.

***

It's late and the train carriage is a gallery of tired faces.

| Not me | not me | not me | not me | not me | not me |

| Not me | not me | not me | not me | not me | not me |

Everyone is very quiet on this train. Everyone except a young man sitting opposite me who's talking loudly on the phone.

It's a disgrace what they're doing to me, a disgrace.

It's sabotage, yeah? Full-on sabotage, they think I can't see that and when I went down there they wouldn't see me without an appointment. I'm at the end of my. I have a degree, I told them I've got a degree I've got a lot to OFFER do you know what I'm saying?

Everyone is holding themselves back in their seats and very intently not looking at him.

A kind of anti-energy, this not looking.

And they told me, they told me yeah that it wasn't real that my SYMPTOMS yeah all the tests yeah they did TESTS and they found NOTHING! And I said, well look again mate! You'll find it if you LOOK AGAIN!

I lean towards him and listen to the phone pressed to his ear. There is no one on the other end of the line.

Yeah. Yeah that's what I told them – I told them that but they didn't listen. I didn't shout. No. I said it real soft I said it real soft. I really tried to be real soft and gentle with them. But they don't know who they're dealing with. They've got no idea who I am. How powerful I am. No idea what kind of force they're messing with, do you know what I'm saying, what kind of MAN I am? Because I am powerful.

He hangs up the phone.

I AM FUCKING POWERFUL!

I am the only one looking at him. He stares right back at me.

And that's when I go.

So easy, like stepping out of the bath, bounce like light off a watch onto the ceiling and down through the top of the man's head and I'm in his body like a trace-paper copy, like a ghost in a new house ready for haunting. I'm looking out of his eyes and down his arms to his hands on his thighs, the nails are short and one nail is painted a bright sky blue and chipped. I sit inside this head and feel the weight of this new body in the seat, feel these feet ache in tight leather shoes. Listen to this heart pound. I sit carefully inside his head like in a stranger's living room and see images I don't recognise of people I don't know.

A face close to this face spitting you're NOT LISTENING and a baby held to this naked chest pink and sleeping and a lamp goes on in the middle of the night and a sleeve wipes this face clean of tears or rain and these arms wrap around another body pull it close and wipe the crumbs from under the toaster and these eyes need the glasses forgotten on a bedside locker this morning. Rub these eyes with these hands. Look out at the woman slumped pale in the seat opposite taking shallow breaths and her eyes are staring back and her hands are curled in fists in her lap.

I am not that man.

I look at the hands in my lap and tell myself they're my hands. My hands curled tight in hers, my hands curled tight in fists my hands. My hands. My hands.

At 4 a.m. I find myself back at my own front door and I'm not the only one.

***

Another actor enters. It's DEREK. ESSIE *and* DEREK *look at one another.*

ESSIE. What are you doing here?

DEREK. Can I come in?

ESSIE. Is – Maura with you?

DEREK. No. She doesn't know I'm here, actually.

ESSIE. Is she okay?

DEREK. Oh yes. Fine. She's making dal.

ESSIE. What?

DEREK. Dal, she's making a big batch of. Look. Is this a – really bad time, or –

Pause.

ESSIE. Come in. Be my guest.

They go into ESSIE*'s kitchen. Suddenly made real.*

DEREK. Well.

ESSIE. Well.

Pause.

It's late, Derek. What's up?

DEREK. I arrived at about ten.

ESSIE. So you've just been sat on my step?

DEREK. Mmm.

ESSIE. Why?

DEREK. I'll explain.

Long silence.

Your birthday's next week.

ESSIE. Yeah?

DEREK. We should do something. With Maura I mean we should all. Go out.

ESSIE. Is that what you came all this way to tell me?

DEREK. No.

ESSIE. What then?

Pause.

DEREK. You. You look.

ESSIE. What?

DEREK. Tired. Really tired.

ESSIE. Thanks mate.

An even longer silence.

Can you spit it out? Whatever it is?

DEREK. I don't. Eh I don't really know the words for it. You know.

ESSIE. No. I haven't a clue. I need words.

DEREK. Course, course.

Pause.

I've been thinking.

He shifts from foot to foot.

Well, it was what you said – the thing you said the other day that got me thinking.

ESSIE. The other day?

DEREK. When Maura and I took you for dinner.

ESSIE. Three months ago.

DEREK. Was that three months ago? Jesus. The weeks.

ESSIE. Yeah.

DEREK. Well – I've been trying to talk to you since then. Been meaning to, and I suppose I've come here because I've not been able to get it out of my head and I wanted to, eh – just to say that, well I, I sort of know what you mean about all that stuff you were saying.

ESSIE. What stuff?

DEREK. About the – chair. You said you felt like – and I well. I mean I sometimes, well I've actually, often enough. Felt like that. What I mean is, I actually, feel like that – all the time Essie. All the – well all the fucking time.

Pause.

And I think – well I came here to say – to tell you – I really think it'll be alright. You'll be. I mean, I dunno do I, what do I know about any of this stuff, but for what it's worth – I think that it might be – it might all be alright.

Long pause.

ESSIE. Christ. You should be a motivational speaker.

Pause.

Derek?

DEREK. Yeah?

ESSIE. Am I real?

Pause.

DEREK. Yes.

Pause.

ESSIE. Okay.

DEREK. Okay?

ESSIE. Okay.

ESSIE *reaches out to* DEREK. *Touches him.*

Okay?

DEREK. Okay.

End of play.

A Nick Hern Book

This revised edition of *Collapsible* first published in Great Britain in 2019 as a paperback original by Nick Hern Books Limited, The Glasshouse, 49a Goldhawk Road, London W12 8QP

First published by Nick Hern Books in *Plays from VAULT 4* in 2019

Cover design by Martha Hegarty; photography by Bronwen Sharp

Designed and typeset by Nick Hern Books, London
Printed in Great Britain by Mimeo Ltd, Huntingdon, Cambridgeshire PE29 6XX

A CIP catalogue record for this book is available from the British Library

ISBN 978 1 84842 839 3